Lighter Than Air

by Johanna Lee

PEARSON

Scott
Foresman

DK

What You Already Know

Matter is anything that has mass and takes up space. There are many ways to identify properties of matter, such as by using your senses or by performing simple tests. The three most familiar states, or phases, of matter are solid, liquid, and gas. The state of matter is determined by the movement and arrangement of its particles.

Matter has properties that can be measured. Scientists use metric units when they measure and compare matter. Mass is the amount of matter in an object. Mass can be measured with a pan balance. Volume is the amount of space that matter takes up. Volume can be measured with a graduated cylinder or unit cubes. Density is the amount of mass in a certain volume of matter.

The cork has the least density of any substance in the container.

Matter can be combined to form mixtures. A mixture is a combination of two or more substances that can be easily separated. The substances have the same properties when they are mixed as they had before they were mixed. A solution is a kind of mixture in which one or more substances are dissolved into another. The substance that is dissolved is the solute. The substance that dissolves the other substance is the solvent. Solubility is the ability of one substance to dissolve into another.

When you make a mixture, you are making a kind of physical change. A physical change is a change in the size, shape, or state of matter. A chemical change occurs when the particles of a substance change to form a new substance.

In this book, you will learn about the changes in the volume and density of air that allow hot-air balloons to rise and fly through the sky.

Introduction

Have you ever seen a brightly colored hot-air balloon float above the treetops? Maybe you wondered how the balloon was able to stay in the air without wings or an engine. The explanation is simple. The air inside the balloon is less dense than the air outside the balloon, and this allows it to rise.

Hot-air balloons consist of three basic parts: a basket, a heater, and the balloon itself. The pilot and passengers ride in the basket that hangs under the balloon. A heater is mounted above the basket and below a small opening in the balloon.

A flame from the heater warms the air inside the balloon. When air is heated, a physical change takes place. The air expands, which makes it lighter than the cooler air outside the balloon. Lighter air rises, so the balloon rises too.

People all over the world enjoy the sport of ballooning.

Other balloons contain gases such as hydrogen or helium. Hydrogen and helium have extremely low densities. How low? Approximately 90 elements occur naturally on Earth. Of them, hydrogen and helium are the least dense.

Earth's atmosphere is composed mainly of nitrogen, with lesser amounts of oxygen and argon. Compared to most other elements, these three gases have low densities. However, they are much denser than hydrogen and helium. Because hydrogen and helium are less dense than the gases that make up our atmosphere, balloons containing them can float.

Balloon Pioneers

More than 200 years ago, people became curious about flight. Two of these people were Joseph Michel and Jacques Étienne Montgolfier, brothers who lived in France. They conducted experiments with paper bags filled with hot air. Their experiments led to the invention of the first hot-air balloon.

Their balloon was a silk bag that was lined with paper. In June, the brothers sent a balloon without passengers into the air. On September 19, 1783, they were ready to attempt the first hot-air balloon flight with passengers. A crowd that included King Louis XVI and Queen Marie Antoinette assembled at Versailles, France, to watch as a sheep, a rooster, and a duck were loaded into the basket below the balloon.

The Montgolfier brothers incorrectly thought that smoke caused the bags to rise.

Pilâtre de Rozier and the Marquis d'Arlandes were the passengers in the Montgolfier balloon.

Ropes were used to keep the balloon from flying away too soon. When the ropes were released, the balloon lifted about 1,500 ft into the air. Several minutes later, the balloon and its passengers landed safely.

Encouraged by the flight's success, the Montgolfiers moved on to the next challenge—a balloon flight with human passengers. In October, 1783, they sent a man eighty feet into the air in a balloon that was tethered to the ground. Then on November 21, 1783, in Paris, two men lifted off in the brothers' balloon. This time, the men would fly free.

The men had to keep a fire burning in order to keep the balloon aloft. After a flight of about 25 minutes, the balloon landed a few miles from Paris, with the men aboard unharmed.

Moving Molecules

The Montgolfiers believed they had discovered a new gas. Naming it "Montgolfier gas," they thought it was less dense than air, and therefore made their balloons fly. But they were wrong. Like modern hot-air balloons, the gas inside their balloons contained neither hydrogen nor helium. In fact, it was no different from the gases that make up the air outside.

The real reason the Montgolfiers' balloon flew was that it used heated air. Air is a gas. The molecules in a gas are spread far apart, and they move around on their own. When air is heated, its molecules move faster. The molecules spread even farther apart. As a result, the molecules of hot air take up more space, or volume, than the molecules of cooler air. This means the density of the air has decreased.

Gas molecules move on their own, but they move faster when heated.

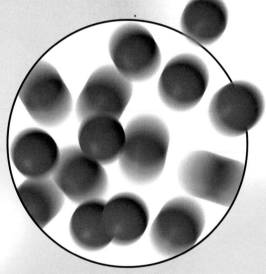

The experiment shown here demonstrates how hot air rises. A bottle with a balloon stretched over its top is placed into a container of water. The water is heated until it becomes warmer than the air inside the bottle. The heat from the water transfers to the air inside the bottle.

The heat forces the air's molecules to move faster and farther apart. In order to do so, they need more space. Where can they find it? The water prevents them from sinking. The bottle blocks them from spreading out. The only way they can escape is by moving up through the bottle's opening. So the warmer air rises and expands into the balloon. This is what happens when the air in a hot-air balloon is heated.

Warm water causes the balloon to expand. What do you predict would happen if the bottle were placed into a container of cold water?

Density

   The density of an object is the quotient of its mass divided by its volume. If objects have the same volume but different mass, the density of the objects is also different. For example, the three balls pictured below have the same volume. However, the mass of the balls is different. The hardwood ball has the greatest mass, so it has the greatest density.

   The density of an object determines whether or not it will float in water or in air. If the density of an object is greater than the density of water, the object will sink. If the density is less, the object will float.

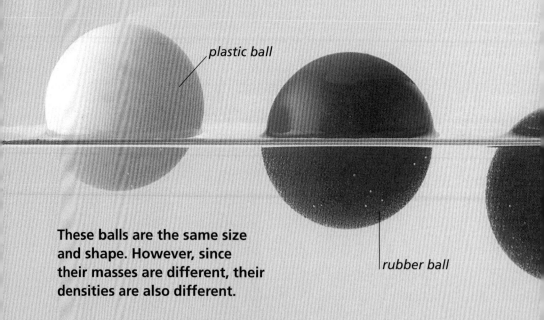

plastic ball

rubber ball

These balls are the same size and shape. However, since their masses are different, their densities are also different.

The human body is about two-thirds water. Overall our bodies are slightly less dense than water. Because of that, we float in water, but just barely.

The picture below of a peeled lemon and an unpeeled lemon shows objects with different densities. The peeled lemon sinks because its density is greater than the density of the water. The unpeeled lemon is less dense than the water because lemon rind is full of air bubbles. So the unpeeled lemon floats.

hardwood ball

The unpeeled lemon floats, while the peeled lemon sinks.

Buoyancy

Buoyancy is the force that allows a ship to float in water or a balloon to float in air. The density of an object determines its buoyancy. An object is buoyant in water if its density is less than that of the water. That means that an object that is denser than water will sink. An object that is less dense than water will float in water.

A scientist in ancient Greece, Archimedes, discovered the law of buoyancy. According to Archimedes, when you place an object into water, the object will displace some of the water. In other words, the object will push the water aside and force it to move somewhere else.

When an object that is not buoyant in water sinks, it will displace a volume of water that is equal to the volume of the object. For this to happen, the object must be denser than water.

A balloon is buoyant when the air inside it is less dense than the air in the atmosphere. Heating the air inside a hot air balloon decreases its density, making it more buoyant.

The law of buoyancy explains how this ship can float in water.

Air inside the balloon is less dense than air outside. The balloon rises.

Air inside and outside the balloon are equally dense. The balloon stays at the same altitude.

Air inside the balloon is denser than air outside. The balloon sinks.

Fire is used to heat the air in balloons. Unfortunately, fires can cause accidents.

Up, Up, and Away

After the Montgolfier brothers invented the hot-air balloon, ballooning quickly became a popular sport. Colorful balloons of different shapes and sizes could be seen floating in the sky.

The early balloonists faced several challenges. They had to fill the bags of their balloons with hot air while they were still on the ground or carry open fires while they floated. Since hot-air balloons depend on the wind, balloonists had to move in the direction the wind blew. Without a push from the wind, the balloon would just hover in the air. Balloonists became annoyed with not being able to control the direction of their balloons. They tried to figure out ways to move and steer their balloons.

The Rise and Fall of a Balloon

The balloon is filled with hot air. This allows it to rise. When the air inside cools, the balloon comes back to the ground. The air is let out until the next flight.

Airships

Giffard's airship

In 1852, a determined inventor named Henri Giffard built a long, thin, balloon-like vehicle that could be steered. His vehicle was fitted with a steam engine and a propeller. A device called a rudder was used to steer it. Giffard's vehicle was called a dirigible, from a Latin word meaning "to direct." It was the first airship.

Several years later, a German count named Ferdinand von Zeppelin designed airships that were more efficient than the early ones.

During the 1920s and 1930s, airship travel was luxurious.

poster of an airship

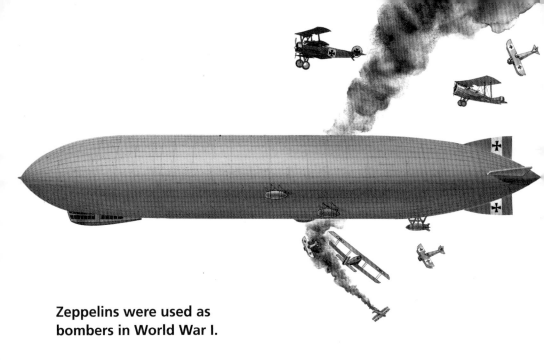

Zeppelins were used as bombers in World War I.

Zeppelin and his team used gas engines to turn the propellers on their airships. Gas engines were lighter than the steam engines used by Giffard. These airships were called zeppelins, after their inventor.

One well-known zeppelin was the *Graf Zeppelin*. This airship was 775 feet long and could fly as fast as 80 miles per hour. The airship flew around the world in less than 22 days.

Airships differed from hot-air balloons in several ways. First of all, airships were much larger, in order to carry passengers and cargo. Also, they were filled with hydrogen rather than hot air. Finally, airships were much more luxurious than hot-air balloons.

Explosive Beginnings

Zeppelins contained hydrogen gas. The advantage of using hydrogen was that it is less dense than air. The disadvantage was that it is highly flammable, which means that it can catch fire easily. In fact, an explosion of a zeppelin resulted in the end of airship travel.

The most famous zeppelin was the *Hindenburg*. It was more than 800 feet long. After its first flight in 1936, the *Hindenburg* made many flights back and forth across the Atlantic Ocean from Germany to America. Unfortunately, on May 6, 1937, the *Hindenburg* burst into flames just as it was about to dock in New Jersey. Although there were survivors, 36 people died in the explosion.

The *Hindenburg* was many times as large as a jumbo jet.

People were horrified when they learned about the *Hindenburg* disaster.

Giants of the Air

Many years have passed since the *Hindenburg* disaster. Airships are being built again. Modern airships still have engines so that pilots can steer them in any direction. However, the new airships are different from the earlier ones in several ways. Their engines are much lighter and more powerful. New materials, such as Kevlar fibers, are used to construct modern airships. The inside of a modern airship's gondola—the cabin in which the pilots and passengers sit—has the kind of communications, control, and guidance systems found in other modern commercial aircraft.

Modern airships, often called blimps, are also much smaller than the airships of the past. Blimps are only about one-fourth the size of the *Hindenburg*. Early airships had frames, but modern blimps do not.

Helium-filled balloons are sometimes used as decorations.

Ballonets, or airbags, line the inside of the airship. They allow the helium to expand safely as the airship climbs in the air.

Another important difference is that the airships of today use helium instead of hydrogen. Helium has a few disadvantages when compared to hydrogen. Although it is much less dense than air, it is denser than hydrogen. This makes it less efficient. Helium is less abundant than hydrogen, so it is also more expensive.

But helium's biggest advantage is that it is safer than hydrogen. Helium will not catch fire. Because of this, laws now require all airships that carry passengers to use helium. Several special systems located within an airship's gondola monitor the pressure of the helium inside of the envelope, or main body, of the airship.

The body of a modern airship is called an envelope.

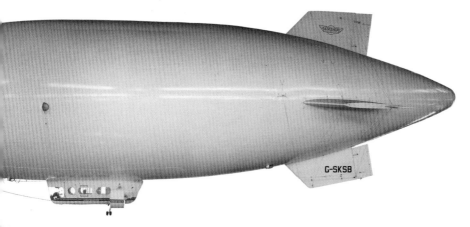

Modern Uses

Several different industries use modern airships and hot-air balloons. Companies use blimps to advertise the brand names of their products. Blimps carry cameras to film sporting events.

Modern hot-air balloons are much like the first ones invented. However, there are some important differences. The new balloons are made of lighter but stronger materials, such as nylon. The balloon uses a special type of cloth at the bottom so that it is unlikely to catch fire or become damaged by the balloon's propane burners, which provide the heat to lift the balloon.

Balloons can travel greater distances than in the past. In 1999, two men flew a hot-air balloon around the world without stopping or refueling. Then, in 2002, a man flew around the world solo in a hot-air balloon!

This airship displays a message to the athletes in the 2000 Sydney Olympics.

Scientists use balloons for research and to forecast the weather. The National Aeronautics and Space Administration, or NASA, sends about 25 scientific balloons into space each year. Although smaller than most hot-air balloons, NASA's balloons carry several tons of equipment and soar 25 miles into the atmosphere. The instruments on the balloons help NASA learn more about the Earth's atmosphere and record data on the stars and planets. The National Oceanic and Atmospheric Administration, or NOAA, also gathers information using hot-air balloons.

More than 200 years after balloons were first invented, people continue to experiment to find more and better uses for balloons and airships.

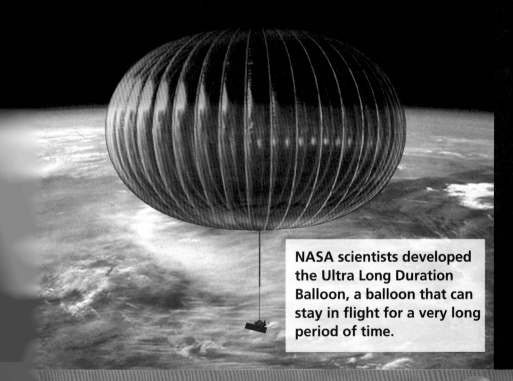

NASA scientists developed the Ultra Long Duration Balloon, a balloon that can stay in flight for a very long period of time.

Glossary

ballonets   the airbags that line the inside of an airship

buoyancy   the force that allows an object to float

dirigible   an airship that can be steered

displace   push away and take the place of

helium   a gas that is less dense than air and does not burn

hover   float in the air

hydrogen   a gas that is less dense than air and can burn